RAKUGO!
Comic Stories from Old Japan

retold by
Ralph F. McCarthy

illustrated by
Yu Takita

KODANSHA INTERNATIONAL
Tokyo•New York•London

Published by Kodansha International Ltd., 17-14 Otowa 1-chome, Bunkyo-ku, Tokyo 112-8652. Copyright © 2000 by Ralph F. McCarthy and Yu Takita, English translation copyright © 2000 by Kodansha International Ltd. All rights reserved. Printed in Japan.

ISBN 4-7700-2426-6
First edition, 2000
00 01 02 03   10 9 8 7 6 5 4 3 2 1

CONTENTS

1. The Other End (*Katabou*)   7
2. The God of Death (*Shinigami*)   27
3. Toku the Boatman (*Funatoku*)   51
4. The Absentminded Messenger
   (*Sokotsu no shisha*)   77
5. Dream Saké (*Yume no sake*)   97

Notes   112

片棒

THE OTHER END
●●●●

Misers go by many names. Tightwad, pennypincher, cheapskate, skinflint…Nowadays we talk about people who are "careful with their money."

Sometimes the richest people are the biggest misers. You've probably heard the story of the wealthy merchant who lived on a great estate with eight servants. One day the merchant began to wonder if having eight servants wasn't an unnecessary extravagance, so he let half of them go. After a while, even four servants seemed more than he needed, so he fired another two. And when the remaining two servants proved perfectly capable of handling everything, it occurred to him that maybe he didn't need any servants at all. Once he'd got rid of the last two and found that he and his wife managed to get by quite well without their help, he started to think he didn't really need his wife either, so he divorced her. Sure enough, he seemed to do well enough on his own, and finally he began to wonder if even he wasn't an unnecessary extravagance. So he hanged himself.

Well, that's an extreme case. But back in the late Taisho era, in Tokyo, there lived another merchant named Kechibei Akanishiya who was almost equally miserly. There was nothing Kechibei hated more than parting with money once he'd got his hands on it. And by working hard and pinching pennies all his life, he'd managed to accumulate quite a fortune.

Back in the late Taisho era...

As for Kechibei's three sons, one might well expect that they'd appreciate all he'd done and would make every effort to increase the family fortune. One might expect that, but it wasn't the case at all. What with drinking, gambling, and womanizing, the three went through the old man's money like water.

Concerned about what might become of his fortune after he died, Kechibei summoned his sons for a talk. The eldest, Kinnosuke, was the first to enter the room.

Kinnosuke: You called, Father? What can I do for you?
Kechibei: Ah, Kin. Come in, son, and sit down. I wanted to ask you something. I know this is rather sudden, but…if I were to die…

> I wanted to ask you something.

Kinnosuke: Father! What a horrible thought!

Kechibei: Now, now, just suppose. Hypothetically speaking…If I were to die, what sort of funeral would you hold for me? I want you to speak freely.

Kinnosuke: Very well, Father, if you insist. Let us suppose that, at some point in the distant, distant future, you should pass on. In that case, I would of course hold a funeral to end all funerals.

> A funeral to end all funerals!

Kechibei: Oh? And what would be so special about it?

Kinnosuke: Well, first of all, it couldn't be held at our shabby little local temple. That would not do at all. We'd rent the great Zojoji Temple in Shiba. We'd serve everyone food, of course, and not just some cheap box lunch. No, no, no. A full-course meal of the finest gourmet cuisine. And naturally we'd provide gifts for each person.

Kechibei: Gifts? Surely there's no need for gifts. It's a funeral, after all.

Kinnosuke: Nothing is too good for you, Father. It's just our way of showing how much you've meant to us. Lacquered boxes full of sweets and delicacies should do. And of course, there'll be guests who've traveled from near and far, so we'll have to provide them all with taxi fare. A little envelope with money in it discreetly attached to each gift…

Lacquered boxes full of sweets and delicacies.

Kechibei: Kin, it's only a funeral, for heaven's sake! No one expects taxi fare.

Kinnosuke: But they shall have it, Father. In beautiful little envelopes with black engraving saying, "With the compliments of the Akanishiya family." And beneath that, the family crest, in gold.

Kechibei: In gold, eh? Good heavens. Well, go on. What about my coffin?

Kinnosuke: Ah, the coffin. Since this is, after all, a once-in-a-lifetime event, the coffin will naturally be of the finest, most expensive material available. Some exotic, fragrant hardwood, polished to a shine, custom-fitted, four inches thick. It'll burn all night long at the crematorium, filling Tokyo with a lovely scent. My goodness, it takes my breath away just to think of it!

Kechibei: Idiot! It takes my breath away, too! Do you have any idea how much a coffin like that would cost? Heaven help us! And just how many guests do you plan to invite?

Kinnosuke: Well, we'd want to keep it on the intimate side. Let's say two thousand or so.

Kechibei: Two thousand? Full-course meals and taxi fare for two thousand people? Are you out of your mind? Oh, my... Very well, away with you! I've heard enough. Obviously I don't dare die while you're still alive! Send in your brother.

Just the thought of how expensive such a funeral would be leaves Kechibei exhausted and feverish. He's panting and wiping the sweat from his brow when his second son, Ginnosuke, enters the room.

Kechibei: Come in, Gin.
Ginnosuke: You wanted to see me, Father?

Kechibei: Yes. Sit down. Listen, son, suppose I were to die…
Ginnosuke: Father!
Kechibei: Never mind, just suppose. What sort of funeral would you hold for me?
Ginnosuke: Funeral, Father? Hmm. Well, as you know, I believe in doing things right. I couldn't possibly be satisfied with just your av-

erage, ordinary funeral. Too dull and gloomy. Your funeral would have to be a magnificent spectacle, something the world has never seen before, a funeral for the ages!

Kechibei: Oh, my goodness! Here we go again!

Ginnosuke: Father?

Kechibei: Never mind. Go on.

Ginnosuke: First we'd have a parade. A great procession of all the most important men in town, marching and singing. That's how we'd start. Then comes the float.

Kechibei: Float? What are you talking about?

Ginnosuke: Oh, not just your average float. We'll have a dollmaker construct a giant figure to look just like you, dressed in a beautiful kimono of the finest silk. This would stand on top of the float. And since you've dedicated your life to keeping your accounts straight, we'd put an abacus in your left hand, and we'd have the dollmaker give your face this ruthless expression, as if you were about to add up someone's bill. Hard-hearted, merciless, like this...Look, Father...

Kechibei: I see you, damn it!

Ginnosuke: Of course you can't have a float without music. A band would be playing from the time we left the house. Drums, flutes... *Boom badda boom! Boom badda boom! Twee, twee! Twee twiddly twee!*

As his father stares at him dumbfounded, Ginnosuke gets up and begins dancing around the room.

Ginnosuke: Boom diddly diddly diddly, boom diddly diddly diddly...Oh, Father, what a beautiful funeral! And we'd rig the doll so it could move in time to the music. *Boom badda boom! Scree, scree! Click click click. Ah! Sproing! Gggyahhh! Mmggg!*

Kechibei: What the hell is that?

Ginnosuke: That's the sound of the doll getting tangled up in telephone wires.
Kechibei: Idiot!
Ginnosuke: Then comes the *mikoshi*!

> Wasshoi!
>
> Then comes the mikoshi!

Kechibei: The *mikoshi*? You mean a portable shrine? At a funeral?
Ginnosuke: Yes, but not just your average portable shrine, Father. This one would hold your remains, in a jar. And we'd have the strongest, toughest men in town carrying it, in case any thugs try to steal the jar.
Kechibei: Why the hell would anyone want to steal my ashes? Whoever heard of such a ridiculous funeral?
Ginnosuke: Think of it, Father! Everyone in

matching *yukata*, marching along with the *mikoshi* and chanting: *Wasshoi! Wasshoi!* And the band playing: *Boom badda boom! Twee tiddly twee! Boom badda boom…*

> Boom badda boom!
>
> Twee tiddly twee!

Kechibei: Quiet, you fool! Enough! Stop, I say!
Ginnosuke: It has to stop at some point, Father, so we can watch the Lion Dance.
Kechibei: Lion Dance? What the…?
Ginnosuke: Oh, not just your run-of-the-mill Lion Dance. The real thing. Two Lion Dance masters in a beautiful, flowing lion suit with a big carved wooden head and movable jaws, winding through the crowd and then climbing a ladder and unrolling a banner that says, "In fond memory of our beloved father, Kechibei

Akanishiya." A hush falls over the crowd, and everyone begins to pray: *Namu Amida Butsu… Namu Amida Butsu…* And then, after a few moments of this reverent silence… *Ssshh-weeee…Bang!* Fireworks! Look, Father, look! They're spelling out your name in fireworks! A-KA-NI-SHI-YA. And just then, three thousand doves are released into the sky! And a blizzard of red and white confetti drifts down! Everyone looks up amazed, thinking, Ah, what a joyous occasion!

Kechibei: Idiot! Get the hell out of here!

Idiot! Get the hell out of here!

Ginnosuke leaves, and Kechibei sits hunched over, his face red and his heart pounding, wondering how he ever came to be cursed with such hopeless, spendthrift sons as these. Tears well up in his eyes and he's muttering to himself, when his youngest son, Tetsunosuke, slides the door open and peeps in.

Kechibei: Who's that? Oh, it's you, Tetsu. Come in, boy. I wanted to ask you something. Not that it matters any more, but…Listen, son, if I were to die…
Tetsunosuke: Yes, Father?

Kechibei: Er…If I were to die, what sort of funeral would you hold for me?
Tetsunosuke: Well, Father, I suppose we'd have to hold some sort of funeral. Not to mention a wake. It's the thing to do, after all.

Kechibei: Yes, yes. So tell me about it. What sort of funeral would it be?

Tetsunosuke: Well, one has to invite a few guests, of course. First and foremost, I'd tell everyone that the coffin was to be taken to the crematorium at ten in the morning.

Kechibei: Ten o'clock? Fine. I don't know why you have to decide the time right now, but... All right. Then what?

Tetsunosuke: Well, we'd actually take the coffin away at eight.

> We'd actually take the coffin away at eight.

Kechibei: Eight o'clock? But then everyone would miss the ceremony.

Tetsunosuke: Exactly. Everyone shows up at ten. "Terribly sorry, but the coffin went two hours ago," I'd tell them. "Oh, what a shame," they'd say. "We so wanted to see him off." Then they'd all just offer a stick of incense and leave. That way we wouldn't have to serve any food or drink.

Hearing this, Kechibei breaks into a broad grin and slaps his knee.

Kechibei: Tetsu, you're a genius! What a brilliant idea! And the coffin…What sort of coffin would it be?

Tetsunosuke: The coffin? Well, Father, the coffin just gets burned anyway. No sense wasting good money on something we're going to burn. I'd get one of the old pickle barrels from the storehouse out back and stuff your body in that. With your permission, of course, Father.

> I'd get one of the old pickle barrels and stuff your body in that.

Kechibei: A pickle barrel? But what about the smell?

Tetsunosuke: Being dead, Father, you wouldn't notice the smell.

Kechibei: Hmm. That's true.

Tetsunosuke: Then there's the padding they use in coffins…

Kechibei: Right, right. You can buy that at the undertaker's, I suppose.

Tetsunosuke: Yes, Father, but I'm sure it's quite expensive. With your permission, I'd like to use old newspapers.

Kechibei: Newspapers? What am I, a fish?

Tetsunosuke: After all, it's just going to burn with the rest of the stuff. And once we close the lid, no one will notice. Of course, it's not

really necessary to use a lid, I suppose, but…
Kechibei: Tetsu, at least have a lid.
Tetsunosuke: Very well. We close the lid, tie ropes around the barrel, and pass a bamboo pole through the ropes to carry it with. No need to rent a hearse.

Kechibei is weeping for joy.

Kechibei: Thank you, son! Well said! Carry me away!
Tetsunosuke: Yes, Father. I'll take one end of the pole, and…

> I'll take one end of the pole.

Kechibei: Yes, son?
Tetsunosuke: Well, I suppose I can hire someone to take the other end.

Kechibei leaps to his feet.

Kechibei: Hire someone? Don't you dare, boy! I'll pop out and carry the other end myself!

死神

THE GOD OF DEATH
●●●●

Poor people generally either have no luck or no ambition, and for Zenhyo it was clearly a case of the latter. Today, as usual, his wife nagged him to bring home some money. And today, as usual, he wandered aimlessly through the streets and failed to find any work or to get his hands on so much as a single copper coin. He wanders back with empty pockets to find his wife waiting for him.

Wife: Well? Where's the money?
Zenhyo: Sorry.
Wife: Nothing? Hmph. And you call yourself a man? What good are you? Why don't you go jump in the river and drown?

> **Well? Where's the money?**
>
> **Sorry, I haven't got any.**

And she starts throwing pots and pans at him. Zenhyo flees back outside, but he's got nowhere to go. He walks along till he comes to the river.

Zenhyo: Some wife I've got! Jump in the river and drown, she says. Well, maybe I'll do just that. That'll teach her! Wait. I remember falling into a well when I was a boy. Swallowing all that water…It was awful. Hell, I'd rather keep on living than have to go through that again. There must be an easier way to die. Something that won't cost any money, of course. Maybe I'll hang myself. If only I knew how…

He's walking along muttering to himself when a voice comes out of nowhere.

God of Death: Let me help you.
Zenhyo: Who said that? Who's there?
God of Death: It's me. The God of Death.

And suddenly a very spooky old fellow appears right before Zenhyo's eyes. He looks about a hundred years old, is wearing a ragged, dirty cloak, and is carrying a long walking stick. No matter how badly you want to die, meeting up with a God of Death can give you quite a start.

Zenhyo: The G-G-God of D-D-D-Death? Get away from me! Get away!
God of Death: Let's talk.
Zenhyo: Talk, nothing! Goodbye!

Zenhyo runs off as fast as his legs will carry him, but the God of Death floats nonchalantly along at his side.

God of Death: Hold up. No use trying to run. You can't get away from me. Listen, how would you like to make a lot of money?

Zenhyo stops running and peers at the old man.

Zenhyo: Money? If I had money, I wouldn't have to die.

God of Death: My point precisely. I can teach you to be a doctor. Lots of money in the medical profession, you know.

Zenhyo: Don't be ridiculous. It takes years to become a doctor. I don't even know how to take someone's pulse!

God of Death: No need to take anyone's pulse. All you need to do is make sick people well. I'll show you how.

Zenhyo: You'd show me how to cure the sick?

God of Death: Sure.

Zenhyo: But why? What's the catch?

God of Death: No catch. I like you. You've got a nice, gloomy nature. And, besides, it's not really your time to die.

Zenhyo: Oh. Well, it's worth a try, I guess. All right, I'm listening.
God of Death: Good. The first thing you must know is that whenever someone has a serious illness, there's certain to be a God of Death sitting near his bed. Human beings can't see him, of course, but I'll arrange it so that you—and only you—can.
Zenhyo: And?
God of Death: Well, it's like this. We gods of death all got together a long time ago and decided exactly where we should sit. If one of us is sitting at the head of a person's bed, behind

Whenever someone has a serious illness, there's certain to be a God of Death sitting near his bed. the pillow, that person's a goner. He or she is going to die, and there's nothing anyone can do about it. But if one of us is sitting at the foot of the bed, there's still hope. All you have to do is get rid of the God of Death by chanting a certain spell. I'm going to teach you this spell, so listen carefully. I'll only say it once: *Ajarakamokuren arujeria tekeretsunopaa*. You chant this, then clap your hands twice—*clap, clap!*
Zenhyo: What was that again? Ajarakamokuren arujeria tekeretsunopaa? And then clap, clap? Is that it? Mr. God of Death? Well, I'll be— he's gone. I guess it worked!

Zenhyo runs home and loses no time hanging a sign on his door that says "DOCTOR." Things start out slowly, however. No one seems to have much faith in a doctor who lives in a shack. Zenhyo and his wife and child continue their life of poverty, and his wife continues to nag him. Then, one day, there's a knock at the door.

Zenhyo: If that's the landlord, come back next week! I'll have the rent for you then.
Servant: I beg your pardon, sir? Is the doctor at home? My master is seriously ill, and we fear he may be dying. We were hoping the doctor could come and take a look at him.

> Is the doctor at home?
>
> Yes, I'm the doctor.

Zenhyo: Oh? Yes, I'm the doctor. I'm rather busy right now, but if it's an emergency I suppose I can fit you in. Lead the way!

So Zenhyo follows the servant to the house of a wealthy merchant. They go into the sick man's room, and Zenhyo sees that, fortunately, a God of Death is seated at the foot of his bed.

Rich man's wife: Is there any hope, doctor?
Zenhyo: Nothing to it. I can cure him in no time.

Rich man's wife: You can?
Zenhyo: Absolutely. Provided you pay me, of course.
Rich man's wife: Name your fee, doctor. No amount of money would be too much.

Well, Zenhyo certainly likes the sound of that. He creeps closer to the sick man's bed, sits up straight, closes his eyes, and begins to chant.

Zenhyo: Ajarakamokuren arujeria tekeretsunopaa. *Clap, clap!*

No sooner has he clapped his hands than the God of Death vanishes. And, lo and behold, the sick man sits up in bed.

Rich man: I'm hungry!
Rich man's wife: Good heavens! Doctor, he says he's hungry! What shall we feed him? Some rice gruel, perhaps?
Zenhyo: Oh, let him have a big bowl of broiled eel or something.
Rich man's wife: Broiled eel! Are you sure it's all right to give him something so rich, Doctor?
Zenhyo: Sure I'm sure. Now, about the money…

Word of this miraculous cure spreads throughout the town, and soon people are beating a path to Zenhyo's door. He goes from one house to another, chanting his spell and clapping his hands, curing patient after patient.

Ajar-kamo-kuren

The money begins to roll in, and Zenhyo promptly divorces his nagging wife and finds himself a young mistress.

What with renting his mistress a fine house, buying her everything her heart desires, taking her on sightseeing trips all over the country, and neglecting his business, Zenhyo is soon penniless again. And of course, once he's used up all his money, he loses the mistress as well.

Zenhyo is soon penniless again.

Zenhyo: Oh, well. Maybe I'm better off alone anyway. No responsibilities…And all I've got to do to get money is to play doctor again.

So once more he hangs the sign on the door, but this time nobody comes.

Zenhyo: Damn! Where are all the sick people when you need them? How am I going to eat?

Just in the nick of time there's a knock at the door. Standing there is the manager of a great estate belonging to the lord of Akasaka.

Manager: Doctor, if you could possibly find the time to take a look at his lordship…

He doesn't have to ask twice, of course. Zenhyo leaps up excitedly and follows the manager to the lord's estate. Once inside, however, he finds to his disappointment that a God of Death is sitting dozing at the head of his lordship's bed. Which of course means there's no hope for the fellow.

The God of Death is at the head of the bed.

Zenhyo: Tsk! What kind of luck is this? The man's going to die. Nothing anyone can do.

Manager: But surely a doctor of your legendary skill can think of something. We're prepared to offer you five thousand *ryo* of gold to save his life.

Zenhyo: Fi–Five thousand? Well, I could certainly use the money, but, look here, he's at the wrong end of the bed.

Manager: I beg your pardon, Doctor?

Zenhyo: I mean, if this were the *foot* of the bed…

> Five thousand ryo of gold!
>
> I could use the money.

As he's saying this, a breeze blows in from the garden, and a dried leaf floats through the open door, spinning slowly as it falls. This gives Zenhyo an idea.

Zenhyo: I've got it! Listen, can you find four healthy young men?

Manager: There are any number of strong young men in service here.
Zenhyo: Four is all we need. Bring them to me.

So the manager fetches four young workers, and Zenhyo positions them at each of the four corners of the sick man's mattress.

> One man at each corner.

Zenhyo: Now, when I give the signal, spin the mattress around. I want you to turn it so his feet are here and his head is there. You follow me? But not till I give the signal.

Zenhyo settles down to wait, watching the God of Death—whom no one else can see, of course. And, just as he hoped, it's not long before the god begins to nod off. Seizing this opportunity, Zenhyo gives the signal, the men turn the mattress around, and Zenhyo hurriedly chants his spell.

Zenhyo: Ajarakamokuren arujeria tekeretsunopaa. *Clap, clap!*

... *tekere tsunopaa*

The God of Death awakes with a start, but it's too late. With a resentful glare at Zenhyo, he disappears.

His lordship recovers, and Zenhyo collects his five thousand *ryo* and heads for home. On the way, he stops for a few drinks to celebrate, finally stumbling out into the street much the worse for wear and very full of himself indeed.

Zenhyo: Ha! That sure worked out well. Ha,

ha! What a face that old God of Death made when he saw how I'd tricked him!

Just then he hears a voice he seems to recognize.

God of Death: Zenhyo...You fool!
Zenhyo: Eh? Who's that? You'd better watch your mouth, pal. Come here, and I'll show you who's the fool!
God of Death: Who do you think you are, pulling that trick on me?

And out of the shadows steps the same God of Death he met that night by the river.

Zenhyo: Oh, my! It's you! You mean you were the one I just tricked? Hey, no hard feelings! How was I to know? All you gods of death look more or less alike, and it was pretty dark in that room...

God of Death: I don't want any excuses. Come with me!

The God of Death who treated him so kindly before is now as angry as the devil. He grabs hold of Zenhyo's collar and begins dragging him along.

Zenhyo: Wait...Wait a minute. Forgive me. I was on the verge of starvation. Have a little mercy, please. Hey! Where are you taking me?
God of Death: You'll see. Come along. We're going down these steps.
Zenhyo: Steps? Where did these steps come from? I never noticed them before...Hey, it's dark down here. Where are we?

> Down these steps.
>
> Where are we?

God of Death: Never mind. Quit dragging your feet. Here, take my walking stick. Come on, now. Quick!

The god of death pulls Zenhyo along in the darkness until the steps end and they're in a cavern of sorts.

Zenhyo: What's this? It's bright all of a sudden. Well, no wonder. Look at all those candles! Kind of pretty. What are they for?
God of Death: Those candles are the lives of human beings.
Zenhyo: Really? There are all kinds, aren't there? Long ones, short ones…

There are all kinds, aren't there? Long ones, short ones...
Those candles are the lives of human beings.

Zenhyo's eyes fall on one particular candle, an exceptionally long one shining more brightly than the rest.

Zenhyo: Who's life is that, Mr. God of Death?
God of Death: Interesting you should pick that one out. That, Zenhyo, is the life of your son. The boy you've neglected all these years.
Zenhyo: You don't say! So he's still going strong, is he? And that one behind it, the one about half burned down and smoldering?
God of Death: That's your ex-wife.
Zenhyo: Well, that explains the smoldering. What a temper that woman has! And the one next to it? That little bitty stub of a candle. It looks like it's just about to go out. Who's life is that?
God of Death: Yours, Zenhyo.
Zenhyo: What did you say? That candle is my life? But it's almost finished!
God of Death: That's right. And when it goes out, you die.
Zenhyo: Don't say that! I can't be about to die! Look how healthy I am!
God of Death: When it goes out, you die.
Zenhyo: You're serious, aren't you? But it's

going to go out any minute now! Mr. God of Death, please do something! Don't let it go out! I can give you five thousand *ryo*...
God of Death: That money was your downfall, Zenhyo. Your life was originally going to be much longer. But you got greedy and traded your life-span for that of his lordship. Once you've switched lives with someone, there's no going back.
Zenhyo: Come on, there must be something you can do! I'm begging you!

Zenhyo falls to his knees, tears rolling down his cheeks, and throws his arms around the God of Death's legs.

God of Death: What a crybaby! All right, look, here's another candle stub. If you can light it from your own candle, your life will be that much longer.
Zenhyo: Quick! Give it to me!

Zenhyo takes the stub from the God of Death and tries to light it with the flickering flame on his candle. But he's so frightened that his hands are trembling uncontrollably and he can't get it lit. The God of Death watches him with a cold smile and decides to tease him.

God of Death: You'd better hurry! It's going out! The flame's going out! Quit trembling like that, you coward!
Zenhyo: Quiet! Can't you see I'm trying to concentrate?
God of Death: Hurry! Look, it's starting to sputter! If it goes out, you die! It's going out! It's going…Ooops!

船德

TOKU THE BOATMAN
● ● ● ●

Tokusaburo, the only son of a wealthy family, has been disowned by his parents for being a playboy and a ne'er-do-well. Having nowhere to go, he takes up residence at the Daimasu Boathouse in Yanagibashi. Freeloading off the people who run the boathouse and are indebted to his father for one reason or another, he spends his days doing absolutely nothing.

In most cases, when a young master is disowned he eventually comes to his senses. Seeing the error of his ways, he settles down, finds suitable employment, and returns to the family's good graces. Tokusaburo is a special case, however. He's never worked a day in his life,

> Tokusaburo is a special case…

and it has never even occurred to him to look for a job. Until one afternoon…

Toku: Ah, I'm so bored. It's not bad lying around all day like this, gazing at the river, but it does get boring. What was that dream I had last night? A sea bream wearing shoes…Boring! I ought to find something to do. Maybe I should become a boatman! I'll talk to the Captain.

He goes to see the owner of the Daimasu Boathouse.

Toku: Captain, I've got a favor to ask.
Captain: Now what?
Toku: I'd like to become a boatman.
Captain: You? Ha! Come back when you've

put on fifty pounds of muscle. Listen, son, being a boatman may not look difficult, but think about it. Imagine what it's like in winter, for example. Rowing up and down the river in a straw raincoat, frozen to the bone. Forget it, kid. You don't know how hard a boatman's life is.

Toku: Oh, come on. How hard can it be? Am I not a man?

Captain: Don't make me answer that, son.

Toku: Well, if you refuse to train me, I guess I have no choice. I'll go to work as an apprentice at another boathouse, and once I've learned the ropes I'll come back and work for you.

Captain: Oh, hell, if you're really set on it—

and willing to work for free—you might as well start here, where I can keep an eye on you. I suppose the only thing that'll cure you is actually seeing how tough this work is. I'll call the others and tell them we're taking you on.

The captain summons his boatmen, a rough and tumble crew of muscular young men.

Boatmen: What's that? The young master wants to be a boatman? That's a good one! I can just see him standing at the helm with an oar in his hand. Imagine what a dashing figure he'll cut! Why, he won't be able to beat the ladies away with a stick! Ho, ho, ho!

Captain: Fools! He doesn't even realize you're teasing. I was hoping you'd try to talk some sense into him, but I guess we're stuck with him now.

So Toku begins training as a boatman. The first time out on his own he sinks the boat. Not exactly born to row. He works hard, but as the months go by he doesn't seem to make any progress at all.

Summer arrives, and with it comes the Festival of 46,000 Days. Two gentlemen are strolling beside the river in the direction of Sensoji Temple.

Gentleman A: Hot, isn't it? Too damned hot.
Gentleman B: It is hot, yes. But it's not the heat I mind so much as the—
A: The humanity, yes, I know. Quite a turnout

today. Phew! Look at all this dust. Dusty, hot, crowded, everybody sweating—it's like a human mudslide. What say we take a boat?

B: Absolutely not. I hate boats. They frighten me.

A: Don't be silly. Try it once and you'll love it. Fresh air, cool breezes blowing as we float lazily down the river puffing on our pipes. We get to our destination well rested and with a healthy appetite. Food tastes better, saké is sweeter...Yes, we'd best take a boat.

B: Not on your life. I hate boats, I tell you.

A: Oh, come. You've heard the expression "Hell lies just under the planks"?

B: "Hell lies just under the planks"? You have an odd way of trying to convince a fellow!

A: Well, just think about it. The reverse must also be true—Heaven lies just above the planks! It all depends on how you look at things, you see. Look, here's the Daimasu Boathouse now. I've used them any number of times. And wait till you see the lady of the house. What a beauty!

B: Presumably we'll be boarding a boat, not the lady of the house.

A: You jest. In rather poor taste, I might add. Good afternoon, madam!

Captain's wife: My, what a pleasant surprise!

A: Wonderful to see you again! We're on our way to the festival, don't you know. My friend here is a bit reluctant, but I'd like to treat him to a boat ride.

Wife: Oh, dear. I wish we could help you, but I'm afraid we have no boats left.
A: But there's one docked right there.
Wife: Yes, there's a boat, but no one to row it. Even my husband is out on the river with clients today.
A: Even the Captain, eh? Bad luck! I guess everyone has the same idea on a day like this.

Just then, however, the gentleman happens to notice Tokusaburo slumped against a pillar, dozing.

A: Hold on. Isn't that a boatman?
Wife: Who, Toku? Well, he's a boatman of sorts, yes, but…
A: Already booked? But that's all right. We're

only going as far as the pier near the temple. He'll be back in no time. I say, young man! Young man!

Toku awakes with a start and looks about him, blinking.

Toku: Huh? Wha—? Oh. Hello there.
A: Can you take us out in that boat?
Toku: Who, me? Yes! Of course! You betcha!

Who, me?

Toku leaps up, but the Captain's wife stops him.

Wife: No! Tokusaburo, you mustn't! This is a very important client. We simply can't afford to risk it!
Toku: But, missus—

A: Madam, please! You're willing to take us, young man, isn't that so?
Toku: Why, there's nothing I'd rather do! Please, missus, please let me take them!
Wife: But Toku…
Toku: Please please please please please?
B: I don't like the looks of this. He seems awfully odd…
A: Don't worry. He's still half-asleep, that's all.
Wife: Toku, you're sure you can handle this?

> Please please please please please?
>
> You're sure you can handle this?

Toku: Absolutely! I promise I won't tip the boat over again.
B: "Again"? Did you hear that? I'm leaving!
A: Where's your sense of humor? A typical boatman's jest, nothing more. Everything's going to be fine. Isn't that so, young man?
Toku: You betcha! If you gentlemen will just

step into the boat there, I'll go make the necessary preparations.

So Toku dashes off, and the two gentlemen walk out on the dock. One gets in the boat and helps the other aboard.

A: Careful. Here, take my hand. Easy! There you go. Sit down right here and try to keep still. That's it. See? You feel better already, don't you? There's nothing quite like being on the water. The breeze, the rippling waves…

B: You keep saying that. Personally, I much prefer having my feet on solid ground.
A: Relax and enjoy. You're going to love it, I tell you.
B: I'll be happy to survive it. Doesn't that fel-

low look a bit frail to you? More like an actor than a boatman, I'd say.

A: Will you please stop worrying about every little thing? I'll admit he's a tad on the slender side, but it doesn't take muscle to be a boatman—only skill and experience. I'm sure he knows this river inside and out.

B: That's exactly what frightens me.

A: Don't be silly. I wonder what's keeping him, though. "Necessary preparations," he said. Ah, here he comes. What took so long?

Toku: I was just having a quick shave.

A: A shave? Did you hear that? He keeps his customers waiting while he gets a shave. All is vanity, as they say. Let's go, shall we?

Toku: Certainly. Just let me…Oops!

Wife: You're sure you want to do this?

A: Of course we're sure.

Wife: Well, all right then. I'll be praying for you!

Tokusaburo begins pushing with the pole for all he's worth, but they don't seem to be moving.

Toku: Yo! Yo! Yo! Yo!

A: Young man.
Toku: Yo! Ho! Yo! Ho!
A: Young man!
Toku: What?
A: You might try untying the rope.
Toku: Huh? Oh, right. Ha, ha! The rope, of course. There, off we go. Ho! Ho! Ho! Yo! Ho! Ho!
A: Keep quiet, will you? Put down the pole and take the oar now, for heaven's sake. The oar!

> Keep quiet, will you?
>
> Ho! Ho! Ho! Yo! Ho! Ho!
>
> Toku unties the boat, and off they go...

Toku: Patience! Where would a boatman be without his pole? Yo! Yo! Yo! Oops. Lost the pole.

With the pole stuck in the mud some way upstream, the boat begins slowly spinning.

> Take the oar now.
>
> Patience! Oops. Lost the pole.

A: I say, boatman! We seem to be going around in circles.
Toku: Yes, well, that always happens. This boat likes to circle three times before settling in.
A: Three times? What is it, a boat or a dog?

At last they drift out into the current and head downstream. Toku takes hold of the oar, grunting and groaning as he struggles with it. Zigzagging erratically, they soon come to a bridge. Standing on the bridge is a local bamboo merchant. He gawps down at them and waves his arms excitedly.

Toku: Yoo-hoo! Mr. Bamboo-man! Look at me! I'm taking these clients to the pier!
Bamboo-man: Don't do it! Go back! Go back!

B: Why did he say "Go back"? He seemed rather distressed...Look, I've had enough. Let me off.

A: Relax, will you? Enjoy the scenery. Everything's going to be fine, isn't it, young man?

Toku: Oh, sure. I tell you, though, a fellow makes one little mistake, and they never let you forget it.

B: Mistake? What mistake?

Toku: Oh, nothing, really. One of my passengers happened to be thrown from the boat a while ago. No one would have made such a fuss if she hadn't had that baby strapped to her back...After all, I fell in the water, too. It's not as if I wanted it to happen.

B: Wait! Take me to shore! I'm getting off!

A: Stop panicking, will you? Surely it was just

> Wait! Take me to shore!

a freak accident. Nothing like that has happened recently, has it, young man?
Toku: Certainly not. I've lost a few clients, but I myself haven't fallen in once since then.
B: Let me out of here!
A: Calm down. He's just joking.
B: Some joke. I say, boatman, can't you keep to the middle of the river? We're heading right for that stone embankment. Be careful!
Toku: It happens all the time. It's the strangest thing, but this boat seems to be irresistibly attracted to that stone embankment. Nothing I can do about it.
A: This boat has a mind of its own, does it? That's more than I can say for the boatman. Watch out! We're going to hit…Oh, hell, now we're stuck.

Toku: You're right. We've stopped moving.
A: Well, do something! We can't stay on these rocks all day.
Toku: That's easy for you to say. Listen, do you want to take the oar and try rowing this thing?
A: If I knew how to use an oar I wouldn't have hired you in the first place!
Toku: All right, then, keep quiet, will you? Hey, mister, what's that you've got in your hand? An umbrella? Well, use your head, man! Push us off the rocks with it.
B: With my head?
Toku: With your umbrella! What else are we going to use? We lost the pole, remember? What are you waiting for?
B: How did I get into this mess? All right. I'll try. Some boat ride!

Groaning and muttering, the gentleman sticks the tip of his umbrella in a crack between the stones and pushes. Finally the boat pulls free and drifts out into the current again. However…

B: My umbrella! It's stuck in the rocks! Boatman! I say, boatman! We can't leave my umbrella behind!

Toku: Too late! It's not as if we can go back for it.
B: But it's right there!
Toku: Well, what do you want me to do? Goodness, you act as if you're the first person ever to lose an umbrella. Take another look at that embankment. Umbrellas, swords, canes, fans…Nine out of ten of my customers leave something behind.

The boat begins rocking violently.

They've scarcely made it to the middle of the river again when the boat begins rocking violently.

B: What's going on?
A: Awfully rough ride. I say, young man, you needn't paddle so hard!

The gentlemen look back to see Toku with his eyes tightly shut, rowing frantically.

Toku: I can't see!
A: Well, open your eyes!
Toku: I can't!

A: Why not?
Toku: Sweat is dripping into them! I can't see a thing! Listen, if a big boat comes along, push it out of the way.
A: How are we supposed to do that?
B: Get a grip on yourself, young man! Now what are we going to do? I told you I didn't want to ride in any damned boat!

A: Young man! Young man!
Toku: Ah…Ahhh…I can't go on. I'm exhausted.

To the two gentlemen's utter astonishment, Tokusaburo collapses.

A: What do you mean, you can't go on? Don't be absurd. Stand up, damn it!
B: This is hopeless. He can't row, you can't row, and I can't row. We're done for! I told you I hate boats! Help! Help!

> *I hate boats! Help! Help!*
>
> *Stand up, damn it!*

A: Calm down. I say, young man, look here. The pier's just ahead. Surely you can get us that far. Get a hold of yourself!

> The pier's just ahead. Get a hold of yourself!

Toku: I can't. It's all over... We're going to die. Oh! Mother! Mother!
A: I don't believe it. Now he's calling for his mother. I must say, this is all most unpleasant.
B: Unpleasant, my foot! At this rate we'll drift out to sea! What are we going to do?
A: I suppose we'll just have to get out and wade to the pier.
B: You mean jump in the water? Not on your life. You're the one who got us into this. I told you I didn't want to take a boat. You get out. You can carry me to shore.
A: All right. It's shallow here. Look, you can see the bottom. Here we go. Ooh! Kind of chilly. Hop on, then!

> Here we go. Hop on!

As one gentleman digs his feet into the riverbed, the other climbs on his back.

A: You've got an awfully big ass, you know that? What good is a big ass on a man?

> You've got an awfully big ass.

B: My ass is none of your concern.
A: It is when I'm carrying it!
B: Never mind that. Just watch your step, will you?
A: All right, hang on. Here we go. Oops! Sorry. It's a bit deeper here.

Slowly making their way toward the pier, the two gentlemen turn to look back at Tokusaburo. He's still lying at the helm, huffing and puffing.

A: I say, young man! Are you going to be all right?

Toku looks up in a daze.

Toku: Ah! Mister!
A: What is it?
Toku: When you reach shore…
A: Yes?
Toku: Could you hire a boatman to come and get me?

ダブン

Could you hire a boatman to come and get me?

粗忽の使者

THE ABSENTMINDED MESSENGER
● ● ● ●

Long ago, at the castle of the daimyo Lord Sugidaira no Masame-no-Sho, there lived a samurai named Jibuta Jibuemon. Jibuemon was a faithful retainer and a fearless warrior, but he was also absentminded in the extreme and forever making outrageous blunders. This only endeared him all the more to the tolerant Lord Sugidaira, however.

One day the daimyo was in need of someone to take a message to one of the fiefs . And for some reason he decided to send Jibuemon to deliver the message. Informed that his services were required as a messenger, Jibuemon came scurrying out into the courtyard.

Jibuemon: Foodman! Where's the foodman?
Footman A: "Foodman"? What is he, hungry?
Footman B: Heh, heh. What are they thinking, sending a scatterbrained fellow like this to deliver a message?
Jibuemon: Foodman! Foo…Eh? That's not right. Foo…foo…footman! That's it! Where's the footman?
Footman: At your service, sir.
Jibuemon: Bring me a cow at once.
Footman: A cow, sir?
Jibuemon: Not a cow, a whatchamacallit… That thing you ride.
Footman: If it's a horse you want, sir, I have one right here, all ready to go.
Jibuemon: Horse! That's it! Let me just…Wait a minute. This is the smallest horse I've ever seen!

Footman: That's a dog, sir. The horse is over here.

Jibuemon: Oh. Yes, that's more like it. Up we go, then. Just a second! What sort of horse is this? It has no head!

Footman: The head is behind you, sir. You got on backwards.

Jibuemon: Backwards? Good heavens, you're right. The horse is pointed the wrong way! Well, I'll just lift my rear end, like this, and you spin the horse around beneath me.

Footman: That won't work, sir.

Jibuemon: It won't? All right, then, I guess we have no choice. Cut off its head and stick it on this end.

Footman: Please, sir. It'll be much easier if you just dismount and get back on.

> *Jibuemon makes his way to Lord Akai's.*

Jibuemon finally gets mounted correctly and makes his way to the estate of Lord Akai, where he's shown into a waiting room. He's greeted there by an elderly samurai.

Sandayu: Good afternoon. Allow me to introduce myself. I'm Nakata Sandayu, at your service. I'm honored to meet you, sir.
Jibuemon: The honor is mine. Allow me to introduce myself. I'm Nakata Sandayu…
Sandayu: Sir?
Jibuemon: I mean, I'm Jibuta Jibuemon, retainer of Lord Sugi…um…Sugi-something-or-other…Sugidaira, that's it. I'm Lord Sugidaira …No, wait…
Sandayu: I'm honored to meet the illustrious Jibuta Jibuemon.

Jibuemon: That's it!
Sandayu: Quite. And the message you've come to deliver?
Jibuemon: Huh?
Sandayu: The message…
Jibuemon: Message? Oh, right, the message. The message I've come to deliver is…Ooh…
Sandayu: Sir?
Jibuemon: The message I bring is…Ooh… Ahh…
Sandayu: Are you all right, sir?
Jibuemon: I'm fine. But it grieves me to inform you that…
Sandayu: Yes?
Jibuemon: I've forgotten what the message was.
Sandayu: You jest.
Jibuemon: No. Completely slipped my mind.

> *I've forgotten the message.*

They say that we samurai are all one, right?
Sandayu: Yes.
Jibuemon: Well, then, can *you* remember the message?
Sandayu: I'm afraid not.
Jibuemon: Oh? So you're as absentminded as I am. All right. I wonder if you might condescend to allow me the use of a private room.
Sandayu: Certainly, but may I ask for what purpose?
Jibuemon: To commit hara-kiri, of course.
Sandayu: Hara-kiri?
Jibuemon: I have no choice. I've failed in my duty.
Sandayu: Yes, but surely there must be some means of remembering. It would be a shame for a fine samurai like yourself to throw his life

away over a mere lapse of memory! Isn't there anything we can do?

Jibuemon: Well, there is one thing that might help me remember. But I can hardly impose upon you to...

Sandayu: Nonsense. We samurai are all one, as you said. We must help one another. I'll do whatever I can.

I can hardly impose upon you to...

We samurai are all one.

> I beg your pardon?
>
> Pinch my ass. It stimulates my memory.

Jibuemon: Well, then, if you would condescend to apply digital pressure to the flesh of my humble posterior...
Sandayu: I beg your pardon?
Jibuemon: Pinch my ass.
Sandayu: Pinch your...?
Jibuemon: Ever since I was a child, I've found that a painful pinch of my hindquarters can stimulate my memory.
Sandayu: But, but, but...
Jibuemon: Thank you.

And Jibuemon bends over and rolls up his kimono to expose his hairy rear end. Sandayu edges hesitantly forward, reaches out, and tentatively pinches the flesh.

Sandayu: How's that?
Jibuemon: How's what? I don't feel anything.
Sandayu: No? And now?
Jibuemon: Nothing.
Sandayu: All right, then, I won't hold back this time. Mmngg! Did that hurt?
Jibuemon: Did what hurt?

> Did that hurt?

> Did what hurt?

Sandayu: Good heavens! This is the hardest posterior I've ever encountered!
Jibuemon: Thank you. I'm rather proud of it. It's the one part of my humble person that requires no armor in battle. I've been having it pinched since I was a child, after all. It's one big callous. Keep trying.
Sandayu: I'm afraid it's beyond my feeble powers to pinch any harder than this. Perhaps I can find a stronger man to help. Would you

> *Keep trying.*
>
> *How's that? How's that?*

mind waiting here while I ask among our younger samurai?
Jibuemon: Not at all, not at all. Take your time.

Meanwhile, a carpenter named Tamekko, standing in the garden outside, has observed this entire exchange through the open door to the veranda. Once he's stopped laughing, he begins to feel sorry for poor Jibuemon and decides to help. He walks over to where his partner is working and tells him the whole story.

> *What's so funny, Tamekko?*
>
> *Ha, ha, ha! Listen to this!*

Tamekko: Anyway, this samurai fellow has an ass as hard as a rock. Hand me those pliers.
Partner: What are you going to do?
Tamekko: I'm going to pinch his ass with these and save his life!

> I'll pinch his ass with these!

Partner: Tamekko, you fool, don't go getting mixed up in this business. That's just asking for trouble. Besides, you'll rip a hole in his ass with those things!
Tamekko: Well, having an extra hole in the ass is better than slicing open your belly, ain't it? That hara-kiri stuff kills you, y'know!

Tamekko conceals the pliers in his coat and hurries back in time to intercept Sandayu, who's had no luck finding anyone among the proud samurai in his clan willing to stoop to pinching a stranger's hindquarters.

> Tamekko hurries to intercept Sandayu.
>
> What is it?

Tamekko: Nakata-sama!

Sandayu: What is it, carpenter? I'm very busy at the moment.

Tamekko: I know. Busy pinching that idiot's ass, right?

Sandayu: What? How dare you!

Tamekko: Now, now, don't get all huffy on me. I happened to hear the whole thing. I'm here to help.

Sandayu: You? Do you have extraordinary strength in your fingers?

Tamekko: Do I? Why, I was pulling nails out of boards with my bare hands before I could crawl!

Sandayu: You don't say! Hmm…I suppose it's worth a try. But we can't insult the man by having a commoner perform such a delicate operation. Come with me. We'll dress you up as a samurai.

And that's exactly what they do. Tamekko is dressed in a proper samurai outfit and brought back to the corridor outside the waiting room.

Sandayu: What's your name, carpenter?
Tamekko: Tamekko.
Sandayu: Tamekko? What sort of name is that?
Tamekko: It's the only one I've got.
Sandayu: Well, we have to come up with something better than that. You'll be, let's see…Tanaka Tamedayu. Got that? All right, now wait here till you hear me call your name. And watch your language, by the way. Try to sound refined. Use words like "honorable" and "humble" and…

Tamekko: Don't you worry. I know how to put on airs when I have to.

Sandayu enters the waiting room, and Jibuemon looks up at him with mild surprise.

Jibuemon: Who are you?
Sandayu: Don't tell me you've forgotten already. I'm Nakata Sandayu…
Jibuemon: Of course! I remember now. You went to find someone to pinch my…
Sandayu: Precisely.
Jibuemon: Well?
Sandayu: I've found just the man. He has the strength of ten in his fingers, and he's waiting outside the door. If I may introduce—ahem!—our loyal retainer, Tanaka Tamedayu.

Sandayu turns to look at the door, but nothing happens.

Sandayu: I say, our loyal retainer, Tanaka Tamedayu. Tanaka Tamedayu! TAMEKKO!
Tamekko: Yes, yes, hold on, here I am. Pleased to make your humble acquaintance. I'm the honorable Tanaka Tamedayu.
Jibuemon: Quite, quite. The honor is mine.
Tamekko: Leave us, Nakata.
Sandayu: What?
Tamekko: Scram. I can't work with you here, breathing over my honorable shoulder.
Sandayu: Very well. I'll be waiting just outside the door. Call me when he remembers!

Tamekko: You bet. Phew! I thought he'd never leave. All right, buster, stick it out.
Jibuemon: I beg your pardon?
Tamekko: Show me your ass, dammit. I haven't got all day.

Something about this samurai's manners doesn't seem quite right, but Jibuemon can't put his finger on what it is. He shrugs, turns around, bends over, and hikes up his kimono. Tamekko, meanwhile, is taking the pliers from his sash.

Tamekko: Whoa. That's one nasty-looking ass you've got there. Well, here goes…Do you feel that?
Jibuemon: Yes. Yes, I perceive a slight tickling sensation…
Tamekko: You're kidding. All right, then, I'll have to use a little more muscle. Mmph. How's that?
Jibuemon: Oh, yes, I feel that. A little harder, please.
Tamekko: Harder? Good grief! If I'm not careful I'll break my pli…uh, fingers. All right, pal, you asked for it…Grrrr!

> A little harder.

> Harder? Good grief!

> I'll break my pli...uh, fingers.

Jibuemon: Ouch! Yes! Yes, that's very painful! You're awfully strong!

Tamekko: To hell with the compliments! Remember, dammit!

Jibuemon: Ow! It's coming back to me...Keep pinching! Ow! Yes! I remember now!

> OWWWW!

Hearing this, Sandayu bursts into the room.

Sandayu: You remember?
Jibuemon: Yes, it's all come back to me!
Sandayu: And the message?

Jibuemon: That's just it—the message...
Sandayu: What?
Jibuemon: I remember now...
Sandayu: Yes?
Jibuemon: I never asked what it was!

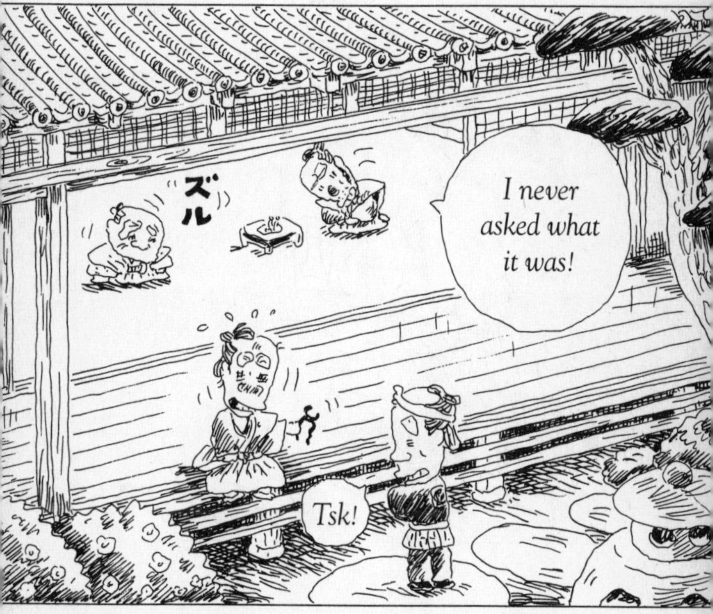
I never asked what it was!
ズル
Tsk!

夢の酒

⑧

DREAM SAKÉ
● ● ● ●

"I'm not the least bit jealous," the wife fumes.

So goes an old *senryu* poem. A little jealousy isn't always a bad thing, but when it gets out of hand, it can cause all sorts of problems.

It's a gloomy afternoon in the rainy season. We're at the estate of the owner of Daikoku-ya, one of the largest department stores in Taisho-era Tokyo. The owner, an elderly gentleman, lives here with his son and the son's wife. The young master has been lying around the house smoking his pipe and finally dozes off, stretched out on the tatami mats.

Wife: Wake up, dear. You'll catch your death of cold.

Huh?

It's me, silly, you wife.

Young master: Mmph? Heh, heh. Thank you again. That was delicious...
Wife: What are you mumbling about? You're still dreaming. It's me, silly, your wife.
Young master: Huh?
Wife: It's me!
Young master: What the...? Why did you wake me, dammit?
Wife: You needn't get angry. I was worried you might catch a cold.
Young master: Well, you could have thrown a blanket over me, then. Damn! Just when I was getting to the good part.
Wife: What you were dreaming about?
Young master: Hm? Oh, nothing.

Wife: You must have been dreaming something. Tell me about it.

> Better not. You'd get mad.
>
> Why would I get angry?

Young master: Better not. You'd get mad.
Wife: Don't be silly. Why would I get angry over a dream?
Young master: You're sure you won't get mad?
Wife: Of course not.
Young master: You promise? All right, I'll tell you…It was a funny dream. I'd gone to Mukojima on business, and as I was walking through the streets it began to rain. I didn't have an umbrella, so I ducked under the eaves of a big house. I was standing there when the maid comes out and sees me. "Why it's the young master!" she says. Then she calls into the house. "Oh, Madam, the young master of Daikoku-ya is here! The very man you were just talking

> As I was walking through the streets it began to rain.

> "Why it's the young master!" The maid comes out and sees me.
>
> Good afternoon.

about!" So I hear this lovely voice calling back to her, "Well, show him in, Ume, you fool!

Don't let him stand out in the rain!" Well, I didn't want to go in, but I didn't want the maid to get into trouble, either, so...

Wife: Don't tell me you went inside a stranger's house? Goodness! Where are your manners? And then?

Young master: Well, the lady of the house turns out to be this beautiful young woman. Twenty-five or -six, medium height, slender but with curves in all the right places, fair-skinned, with the most charming smile. A real knockout! "I'm so glad to finally meet you!" she says. It seems she's been in the store many times and noticed me there. So she has the maid bring out some dishes and a little bottle of saké.

Wife: Don't tell me you drank saké! But you don't even drink!

Young master: That's exactly what I told her. "Thank you, but I'm a teetotaler," I said. "Unlike my father, by the way, who loves saké. My father would rather drink than eat, but it has never agreed with me." I told her that, but she wouldn't listen. "Just one cup," she says. "It can't hurt. Or is it that you don't like my company?" Well, she kept insisting, so, what with one thing and another, we ended up drinking three of those little bottles and…

Wife: Three bottles! I can't believe this. So then what happened. Eh? What happened then?

Young master: Never mind. That's enough. I knew you'd get mad.

Wife: I'm not the least bit angry. What happened next?

Young master: Well, the rain kept falling, so I couldn't very well leave. The lady had the maid bring her shamisen, and she played some romantic tunes. It was very nice, but pretty soon I started to feel sick. "What's wrong?" she says. "You don't look well." I apologized and told her I had a headache. "Oh, it's all my fault," she says, "for insisting you drink that saké!" Then she calls out to the maid. "Ume!

> Now I'm starting to get a headache.
>
> And then…

Prepare a bed in the guest room!" She takes me into this room and has me lie down under the covers and rubs my back and what have you. After a while I started to feel a lot better. But when I told her that, she said something that gave me a real shock. "Isn't that funny?" she says. "You're feeling better but now *I'm* starting to get a headache. If you don't mind, I'll just lie down next to you." And she slips out of her kimono and…

> I'll just lie down next to you.

Wife: Arrrgghhh! How could you! I didn't know you were that sort of man! You beast! Ahh...Ahh!

The wife starts sobbing and wailing at the top of her voice.

Young master: It was just a dream, for heaven's sake. Hold it down, will you? You'll disturb Father...Oh, hello, Father.
Father: What's going on here? I've never heard such a ruckus! What will the servants think?
Wife: Wah! Waahh!
Father: What is it, O-Hana?

Wife: Forgive me...But your son...Mukojima...Another woman...
Father: What are you talking about?

Wife: He went to Mukojima, and it was raining, and a lady invited him in and served him saké, and then, and then, and then he slept with her!

Father: What! Is this true, son? If so, I'll ask you to leave this house at once!

Young master: Ha, ha, ha!

Father: Oh, you think it's funny, do you? Get out!

Young master: Wait, Father, please. It was just a dream!

Father: A dream? Is that right, O-Hana?

Wife: Yes, Father, but cheating is cheating. It means he has lust in his heart! And I'm sure she was a married woman, with a husband of her own! What if word of this were to get out? It would tarnish the image of our store!

Father: Hmm. That's true, I suppose. You see

what a faithful, devoted wife you have, boy? She's worried about your reputation, that's all. You'd better watch what you dream about from now on.
Young master: Yes, Father.
Father: All right, then…
Wife: Wait! Father, I have a favor to ask of you. Please go to that house in Mukojima and give that hussy a piece of your mind!

> Please go to that house in Mukojima.

Father: Huh? The house in Mukojima? But it was just a dream…
Wife: Yes, Father. You'll have to go to sleep. Lie down here, please. I'll tuck you in.
Father: Ha, ha, ha! Well, all right, I'll try…

The father drifts off to sleep, and the next thing he knows he's standing in front of a house in Mukojima.

Ume: Oh, Madam! The master of Daikoku-ya is here to see you!
Lady: My, what a nice surprise! Come in, come in!

Father: Yes, er, thank you. I wanted to talk to you about my son...Goodness, what a lovely house. I really like what you've done with that alcove...

Lady: Oh, my! Flattery will get you everywhere! Tee, hee, hee! Why, you're every bit as charming as your son, aren't you!

Father: Not at all, not at all. Ha, ha, ha!

Lady: Ume, you fool! Why are you bringing tea? Didn't you hear the young master say that his father loves saké even more than food? Bring saké!

Father: Oh, please don't bother...

Lady: It's no bother at all, really! Ume, hurry up and heat a few bottles of the very best...What? The fire's gone out? Well, light a new one, you fool! I hope you don't mind, sir. This may take a few minutes...

Father: Of course. That's very kind of you. Heh, heh. I just can't bring myself to refuse saké. Ha! What a lot of trouble my love of warmed saké used to cause my dear departed wife! Why, when I was young, if there wasn't a bottle of saké on my dinner tray, I'd pick it up and smash it against the wall! Isn't that terrible? Heh, heh... The saké's still not warm, I suppose?

Lady: I'm afraid it may take a bit longer. If you prefer, I could serve it to you chilled...

Father: Oh, no! I do prefer it warmed up, to tell you the truth. I don't mind waiting ...Er...How long do you suppose...

Lady: What can be keeping that girl? Forgive

me. It's so difficult to get good help these days. Shall I serve you just a cup of chilled saké in the meantime?
Father: No, really, I much prefer it warmed...
Wife: Father! Father, wake up!

Father: Hmph? Oh, no! Don't tell me it was just a dream!
Wife: Did you go to the house in Mukojima, Father?
Father: Yes, I went there, but...Oh, what a waste! I blew it!
Wife: You mean I woke you before you had a chance to scold her?
Father: It's not that. Oh, what an idiot I am! I should have drunk it chilled!

Notes

The Other End（片棒）

p. 7　　2 Misers go by many names. けちはいろいろな名前で呼ばれる。　2 Tightwad, pennypincher, cheapskate, skinflint いずれも「どけち」「しみったれ」「吝嗇家」「倹約家」など、けちを意味する同意語　8 merchant 商人　8 on a great estate 広大な屋敷に　11 an unnecessary extravagance 無用の贅沢　11 let half of them go その半分に暇をだした

p. 8　　3 managed to get by quite well 十分にやっていけた　9 hanged himself 首をつった　12 Kechibei Akanishiya 赤螺屋吝兵衛（赤螺はアッキガイ科の巻き貝で、殻を閉じて開かないところから財布の口を開かないけちの代名詞となっている）　13 miserly けちな　14 parting with money once he'd got his hands on it 一度自分の懐に入った金と別れること　16 pinching pennies 節約に節約をかさねて　17 to accumulate quite a fortune 身代を築いた

p. 9　　1 as for ... ・・・はと言えば　2 (would) appreciate ありがたく思う　5 what with ... ・・・などの理由で　6 womanizing 女遊び　6 went through the old man's money like water 親の金を湯水のように使った　8 concerned about ... ・・・を心配して　9 summoned 集めた　10 Kinnosuke 金ノ助

p. 10　　2 hypothetically speaking もしもの話だが　6 if you insist どうしてもというのなら　8 pass on 死ぬ　9 a funeral to end all funerals 極めつけの盛大な葬式　14 shabby みじめな　15 Zojoji Temple in Shiba 芝の増上寺

112

p. 11   **2** the finest gourmet cuisine 極上の料理   **9** Lacquered boxes full of sweets and delicacies should do. 重箱にごちそうを詰めてお持ち帰りいただきます。   **13** taxi fare 車代   **14** discreetly さりげなく

p. 12   **1** for heaven's sake おいおい   **4** with black engraving saying, ... 黒い字で・・・と記して   **5** with the compliments of ... ・・・より謹呈   **6** the family crest わが家の定紋   **9** coffin 棺桶   **13** some exotic, fragrant hard-wood 異国の、香りのいい堅木（白檀、沈香などの木）   **14** custom-fitted 特別あつらえの   **16** crematorium 火葬場   **16** scent 香り   **19** Idiot! ばか野郎！   **19** it takes my breath away just to think of it! 考えるとたまらない！   **21** Heaven help us! ああ、なんてこった！   **23** keep it on the intimate side 内輪だけにしておく

p. 13   **1** away with you! あっちへ行っとくれ

p. 14   **1** leaves Kechibei exhausted and feverish 吝兵衛さんはどっと疲れて熱も出てきた   **3** (is) panting and wiping the sweat from his brow 息をはあはあさせて、額の汗をぬぐっている   **4** Ginnosuke 銀ノ助

p. 15   **1** gloomy 陰気な   **2** a magnificent spectacle 壮大な見世物   **4** a funeral for the ages とむらいの歴史に残るような葬式   **8** parade 行進（木遣り）   **9** procession 行列   **12** float 山車   **14** dollmaker 人形師

p. 16   **3** keeping your accounts straight 勘定を合わせる   **4** abacus そろばん   **5** ruthless expression 因業な顔   **7** bill 勘定書き   **7** hard-hearted, merciless いじわるな、無慈悲な   **15** dumbfounded あきれはてて   **20** we'd rig the doll so it could move in time to the music 人形が音楽に合わせて動くような仕掛けをつける

p. 17   **1** the sound of the doll getting tangled up in telephone wires 人形が電線にひっかかった音   **9** remains お骨   **10** in case any thugs try to steal the jar どんな悪者が骨壺を取ろうとするかわからないから   **14** ridiculous ばかげた   **15** in matching *yukata* そろいの浴衣を着て

p. 18   2 chanting かけ声をかける   7 the Lion Dance 獅子舞   9 run-of-the-mill ありきたりのな   11 flowing 流れるよう   12 movable jaws 上下に動くあご   13 winding through the crowd お客さんの間を練って歩く   14 unrolling a banner 垂れ幕をばらっと落とす   14 in fond memory of our beloved father 愛しい父の思い出とともに（忌中）

p. 19   1 a hush falls over the crowd 一同しーんと静まりかえる   2 *Namu Amida Butsu* 南無阿弥陀仏   4 reverent silence 厳かな静寂   8 doves 鳩   9 a blizzard of red and white confetti drifts down 紅白の紙吹雪が舞う   13 sits hunched over 背中を丸めて座る   15 how he ever came to be cursed with ... どうしてこんな･･･（情けない浪費家の息子）を持っちまったのか

p. 20   1 spendthrift 金づかいの荒い   1 tears well up in his eyes 目に涙がたまる   2 (is) muttering to himself 独り言を言う   3 Tetsunosuke 鉄ノ助   4 peeps in のぞく   14 wake 通夜

p. 21   4 first and foremost まず手始めに   16 what a shame まことに残念です

p. 22   2 offer a stick of incense 線香をあげる   5 breaks into a broad grin and slaps his knee 大喜びで膝をたたいた   13 pickle barrels 漬物のたる

p. 23   6 padding 詰め物   9 undertaker's 葬儀屋

p. 24   6 hearse 霊柩車

p. 25   1 leaps to his feet 飛び上がる   3 (will) pop out 飛び出す

The God of Death（死神）

p. 27   3 ambition 甲斐性   3 Zenhyo 前表（原作では吉原のたいこもち）   5 nagged him 小言をいう   7 to get his hands on so much as a single copper coin 小銭の一つでも工面する

114

p. 28　1 pots and pans 鍋釜　2 flees back outside 外へ飛び出す　7 That'll teach her! 女房への当てつけに。　8 well 井戸

p. 29　6 spooky 気味の悪い　8 a ragged, dirty cloak ボロボロの薄汚れた着物　11 can give you quite a start びっくりする

p. 30　6 floats nonchalantly along at his side 何気なくふわーっとそばに寄ってくる　11 peers at … …をしげしげと見る

p. 31　3 My point precisely. そのとおり。　4 medical profession 医者　7 to take someone's pulse 脈をとる　14 What's the catch? どういうつもりだ?

p. 32　1 it's worth a try やってみるか　13 at the head of a person's bed, behind the pillow 枕元に

p. 33　1 that person's a goner そういう人は助からない　5 by chanting a certain spell 呪文を唱えて　7 Ajarakamokuren arujeria tekeretsunopaa「あらじゃかもくれんあるじぇりあ、てけれつのぱあ」　9 clap your hands twice —clap, clap! 手を2回うつ、ポンポンだ

p. 34　1 loses no time hanging a sign on his door that says … すぐに…の看板を出す　4 (have) faith 信用する　5 shack ぼろ屋　9 landlord 大家

p. 35　9 Nothing to it. わけもないこと。

p. 36　2 provided you pay me お金を払っていただけるということで　4 name your fee いくらでもおっしゃって下さい　7 creeps closer to … …の方へにじり寄る　12 vanishes 消える　12 lo and behold これはいかに

p. 37　4 rice gruel お粥　5 a big bowl of broiled eel うな丼　12 miraculous 奇蹟的な　13 are beating a path to … …に殺到した

p. 38　1 roll in 儲かる　2 promptly すぐに　3 mistress お妾さん　7 neglecting his business 仕事もせずに

p. 39　1 Damn! 弱ったな、こりゃ!　3 just in the nick of

time ちょうど折りよく　**5** the lord of Akasaka 赤坂の殿様　**12** dozing 居眠りして

p. 40　**1** Tsk! チェッ！　**3** a doctor of your legendary skill あなた様のような伝説的な技をもつ医者　**5** five thousand ryo 五千両　**14** spinning slowly as it falls ゆっくりくるくるまわりながら落ちた

p. 41　**9** You follow me? お分かりかい？　**14** nod off うとうとする　**14** seizing this opportunity ここぞとばかり

p. 42　**6** with a start びっくりして　**7** with a resentful glare at ... 恨みがましい目で･･･をにらみつけて　**12** stumbling out into the street よろよろと通りへ出た　**12** much the worse for wear 酔っ払って　**13** very full of himself indeed 大得意で

p. 43　**3** a voice he seems to recognize 聞き覚えのある声　**14** no hard feelings! 悪く思わんでくれ

p. 44　**5** collar えり　**8** was on the verge of starvation 飢え死にしそうだった　**9** mercy 情け

p. 45　**5** a cavern of sorts 洞穴のような所

p. 47　**2** exceptionally 特に　**10** smoldering くすぶっている　**14** That little bitty stub of a candle. 小さい使い残りのようなろうそく。　**15** (is) just about to go out 今にも消えそうな

p. 48　**4** downfall 転落　**6** got greedy 欲をかいた　**6** traded your life-span for that of his lordship 自分の寿命を殿様の寿命と取り替えた　**15** What a crybaby! しょうがねえ男だ！　**21** flickering flame ちらちらする炎

p. 49　**2** tease からかう　**5** you coward! 弱虫！　**7** concentrate 集中する　**8** sputter 消える

Toku the Boatman（船徳）

p. 51   2 Tokusaburo 徳三郎   3 has been disowned by ... ···に勘当された   4 ne'er-do-well ごくつぶし   5 takes up residence at ... ···に住む   6 Daimasu Boathouse in Yanagibashi 柳橋の船宿「大桝」   6 freeloading off ... ···に居候する   8 are indebted to his father for one reason or another 徳三郎の父親に何かと恩義がある   12 eventually comes to his senses 最後には気がつく   13 settles down 腰をすえる   14 returns to the family's good graces 親とよりをもどす

p. 52   3 I'm so bored 退屈だなあ   6 sea bream タイ

p. 53   5 straw raincoat 蓑笠   12 apprentice 弟子   13 once I've learned the ropes こつをつかんだら   16 if you're really set on it そこまで言うなら

p. 54   2 keep an eye on you 見張る   5 we're taking you on あんたを仲間にいれる   6 rough and tumble crew of muscular young men 荒っぽくて腕っぷしの強い若い衆   10 at the helm 舵をとって   11 Imagine what a dashing figure he'll cut! 乙な船頭姿ができあがりますぜ！   15 you'd try to talk some sense into him 若旦那を説得する

p. 55   1 we're stuck with him now もう止めさせられない   5 Not exactly born to row. もともと船を漕ぐのにはむいてなかった。   8 Festival of 46,000 Days 四万六千日(浅草の観音様の七月十日の縁日。この日に詣ると一日で四万六千日お詣りしたのと同じご利益があるとされる)   9 are strolling 歩いている   11 Sensoji Temple 浅草寺   15 humanity 人   15 turnout 人出

p. 56   3 human mudslide 人間泥ころがし   12 Not on your life. ぜったいに嫌だね。   14 "Hell lies just under the planks"「板子一枚下は地獄」   16 convince 納得させる

p. 57   1 reverse 反対   6 the lady of the house 女将   8 presumably 思うに   10 You jest. ばかだね。   10 In rather poor taste, I might add. それに、ちょっと悪趣味だよ。

15 reluctant 気が乗らない

p. 58　**3** docked もやって　**10** slumped against a pillar 柱に寄りかかっている　**15** Already booked? 先約があるのかい？

p. 59　**1** pier 桟橋　**4** looks about him, blinking 目をぱちぱちさせて、きょろきょろする　**8** You betcha! もちろんですとも！　**14** missus おかみさん

p. 60　**11** tip the boat over 船をひっくり返す

p. 61　**1** make the necessary preparations 支度をととのえる　**10** the rippling waves さざ波

p. 62　**1** frail か弱い　**4** he's a tad on the slender side 少しばかり細身だが　**7** inside and out 隅から隅まで　**12** was just having a quick shave ひげをあたっていた　**14** all is vanity 色っぽいねえ　**21** for all he's worth 精いっぱい

p. 63　**5** You might try untying the rope. もやいを解いたらどうだい。　**7** off we go 出ました　**12** Patience! ちょっとお待ちを！

p. 64　**6** current 流れ　**7** grunting and groaning ぶうぶう不平をもらしながら　**9** zigzagging erratically あっちへ行ったりこっちへ行ったりしながら　**10** bamboo merchant 竹屋　**11** gawps down at them 呆然と三人を見た

p. 65　**1** seemed rather distressed あわてていたようだ　**12** No one would have made such a fuss if she hadn't had that baby strapped to her back. 女の人が子供をおぶってなきゃ、あんな騒ぎにはならなかったんだが。

p. 66　**1** freak accident めったにないこと　**9** stone embankment 石垣　**11** be irresistibly attracted to ... ・・・が好きでしかたない　**14** has a mind of its own 自分の考えがある

p. 67　**16** How did I get into this mess? こんなことになるとは思わなかった！

p. 68　**2** crack すき間　**3** pulls free (石垣を)離れた　**15** swords 刀　**15** canes つえ　**16** fans うちわ

p. 69 **1** scarcely ようやく　　**2** begins rocking violently 激しく揺れはじめる　　**6** paddle こぐ　　**8** frantically やみくもに

p. 70　**6** get a grip on yourself しっかりしろ

p. 71　**4** to the two gentlemen's utter astonishment 二人の客が呆然としていると　　**5** collapses へたれこんだ　　**6** Don't be absurd. ばかはおよし。　　**9** We're done for! もうおしまいだ！

p. 72　**5** my foot! なんてこった！　　**5** at this rate このままじゃ　　**8** wade 水の中を歩く

p. 73　**1** digs his feet into the riverbed 川底に足をつける　　**3** ass 尻　　**5** is none of your concern あんたに関係ない　　**13** huffing and puffing はあはあ、ぜいぜいしながら

p. 74　**3** in a daze ぼんやりして

The Absentminded Messenger （粗忽の使者）

p. 77　**1** the daimyo Lord Sugidaira no Masame-no-Sho 大名杉平柾目正殿　　**3** Jibuta Jibuemon 地武太治部右衛門　　**4** faithful retainer 忠実な家臣　　**4** fearless warrior 勇敢な武者　　**5** in the extreme 極端に　　**6** outrageous blunders とんでもないへま　　**6** This only endeared him all the more to the tolerant Lord Sugidaira, however. しかしながら、心の広い杉平様にはこのそそっかしささえも、かわいく感じられた。　　**10** fiefs 領地　　**14** came scurrying out into the courtyard あわてて中庭へと進み出た

p. 78　**1** Foodman! Footman（下男）と言ったつもり　　**4** scatterbrained そそっかしい　　**12** whatchamacallit = what do you call it

p. 79　**9** is pointed the wrong way 反対向きになっている　　**10** rear 尻　　**17** dismount 降りる

p. 80　**2** Lord Akai 赤井殿　　**3** (is) shown into ...・・・へ案内される　　**4** (is) greeted (by ...) ・・・の挨拶を受ける　　**6** Nakata Sandayu 中田三太夫　　**15** illustrious 高名な

p. 81　**12** it grieves me to inform you that ... まことに困ったことに…　**17** Completely slipped my mind. まったく失念した。

p. 82　**7** I wonder if you might condescend to allow me the use of a private room. こちらのひと間を拝借つかまつることはできまいか。　**11** to commit hara-kiri 切腹する　**13** (have) failed in my duty 任務を全うできなかった

p. 83　**1** over a mere lapse of memory ちょっと度忘れしたくらいで　**4** But I can hardly impose upon you to ... あなた様にそんなことをして頂くわけには…

p. 84　**1** if you would condescend to apply digital pressure to the flesh of my humble posterior ... 恐れながら、拙者の臀部の肉に指による圧力を加えて頂きますれば…　**5** Pinch my ass. 尻をつねってくだされ。　**8** hindquarters 臀部　**9** stimulate 刺激する　**13** expose 出す　**14** edges hesitantly forward 恐る恐る前へ出る　**14** tentatively おずおずと

p. 85　**5** won't hold back 遠慮しない　**11** requires no armor in battle 合戦でも鎧がいらない　**14** callous タコ　**15** feeble か弱い

p. 86　**4** Tamekko 留ッ子　**5** has observed the entire exchange 一部始終を見ていた

p. 87　**2** pliers やっとこ　**6** don't go getting mixed up in this business こんなことに出しゃばるんじゃねえ　**8** (will) rip a hole 穴をあける　**11** slicing open your belly 腹を裂き開ける　**13** conceals 隠す　**14** in time to intercept Sandayu 三太夫に途中で会うように　**16** clan 家来　**16** stoop かがむ

p. 88　**6** How dare you! 何を申す！　**7** don't get all huffy on me まあそんなに怒らずに　**14** crawl はう　**16** insult 侮辱する　**17** commoner 平民

p. 89　**4** outfit 衣装　**12** Tanaka Tamedayu 田中留太夫　**15** sound refined あかぬけた口をきく

p. 90　　**1** put on airs 気取る　　**10** Precisely. 左様で。

p. 91　　**5** Pleased to make your humble acquaintance. そちらのようなつまらぬものに会えて光栄じゃ。　　**6** I'm the honorable Tanaka Tamedayu. わしは田中留太夫様と申したてまつるもの。(humble と honorable の使い方を取り違えている)　　**11** Scram. ひっこみなされ。

p. 92　　**1** You bet. 確かに。　　**2** buster おっさん　　**2** stick it out さっさと出しな　　**7** can't put his finger on what it is それが何なのかはっきりとは分からなかった　　**9** hikes up まくる　　**11** sash 帯　　**15** perceive a slight tickling sensation ちょっとくすぐったいような気がいたす

p. 93　　**3** To hell with the compliments! お世辞なんか言ってる場合か！

Dream Saké（夢の酒）

p. 97　　**1** jealous やきもちの　　**2** fumes いきまく　　**3** *senryu* poem 川柳　　**7** Daikoku-ya 大黒屋

p. 98　　**1** (will) catch your death of cold 風邪をひきますよ

p. 99　　**3** Better not. やめとくよ。　　**7** Mukojima 向島　　**10** ducked under the eaves of a big house 大きな家の軒下で雨宿りした

p. 101　　**9** slender but with curves in all the right places すらっとしてるんだけど、出るべきところは出ていて　　**10** fair-skinned 色白の　　**11** A real knockout! ホントの美人！　　**19** teetotaler 下戸　　**21** it has never agreed with me 私の方はとんと不調法でして　　**24** Or is it that you don't like my company? それとも私が相手ではお嫌ですの？　　**25** she kept insisting どうしてもと言い張った　　**25** what with one thing and another あれやこれやで

p. 102　　**11** shamisen 三味線

p. 103　　**3** and what have you とかその他いろいろ(してくれた)

p. 104　　**2** You beast! けだもの！　　**4** starts sobbing and wailing at the top of her voice 大声で泣きわめく　　**10** ruckus 騒ぎ　　**12** O-Hana お花

p. 105　**13** cheating is cheating 浮気は浮気　　**14** has lust in his heart 浮気の虫がいる　　**17** would tarnish the image of our store 店ののれんに傷がつく

p. 106　**1** devoted 献身的な　　**9** give that hussy a piece of your mind その腰軽女に小言の一つも言ってやる　　**13** I'll tuck you in. 私が寝かしつけてやります。

p. 108　**4** alcove 床の間　　**5** Flattery will get you everywhere! お上手ですこと！

p. 109　**4** just can't bring myself to refuse saké どうもお酒だけは断わりきれません　　**6** departed wife 死んだ女房　　**13** chilled 冷やで

p. 110　**11** I blew it! しくじった！　　**13** scold しかる

(都留文科大学講師：滝口峯子)

日本わらい話
Rakugo! Comic Stories from Old Japan

2000年2月10日　第1刷発行

著　者　ラルフ・マッカーシー
絵　　　滝田ゆう
発行者　野間佐和子
発行所　講談社インターナショナル株式会社
　　　　〒112-8652　東京都文京区音羽1-17-14
　　　　電話：03-3944-6493（編集部）
　　　　　　　03-3944-6492（営業部・業務部）
印刷所　豊国印刷株式会社
製本所　株式会社堅省堂

落丁本、乱丁本は、講談社インターナショナル業務部宛にお送りください。送料小社負担にてお取替えいたします。なお、この本についてのお問い合わせは、編集部宛にお願いいたします。本書の無断複写(コピー)は著作権法上での例外を除き、禁じられています。

定価はカバーに表示してあります。

© ラルフ・マッカーシー・滝田ゆう © 講談社インターナショナル株式会社 2000. Printed in Japan
ISBN4-7700-2426-6

講談社英語文庫

楽しく読んで英語が身につく

☆印は英語のレベルを表わしています。☆の数が多くなるほどレベルが上がります。
＊印は、原作をもとに英語文庫のために書き下ろした作品です。

海外の作品

著者	No.	作品名	カセット	レベル
ジェフリー・アーチャー	47	十二本の毒矢		☆☆☆☆
ステュウット・アットキン	82	イギリス昔ばなし＊	■	☆
	94	グリム童話集＊	■	☆
	103	ロミオとジュリエット＊		☆☆
	104	人魚姫＊		☆
	113	シンデレラ＊		☆
	121	紅茶の本		☆☆
	125	ピノキオ＊		☆
	133	美女と野獣＊		☆☆
ウィーダ	154	フランダースの犬		☆☆
ダイアン・ウィルシャ	124	エンジェルの世界		☆☆
ジーン・ウェブスター	67	あしながおじさん		☆☆
L・M・オルコット	115	若草物語		☆☆
レイモンド・カーヴァー	45	ぼくが電話をかけている場所		☆☆☆
	108	愛について語るときに我々の語ること		☆☆☆
ルース・スタイルス・ガネット	161	エルマーのぼうけん		☆☆
トルーマン・カポーティ	64	ティファニーで朝食を		☆☆☆
ルイス・キャロル	40	ふしぎの国のアリス	■	☆☆
	91	鏡の国のアリス		☆☆
ボブ・グリーン	50	チーズバーガーズ		☆☆☆
	111	アメリカン・ビート		☆☆☆
アガサ・クリスティ	127	アガサ・クリスティ短編集	■	☆☆☆
	142	ポアロの事件簿		☆☆
	145	ミス・マープルの事件簿		☆☆
パトリシア・コーンウェル	98	検屍官Ⅰ		☆☆☆☆
	99	検屍官Ⅱ		☆☆☆☆
J・D・サリンジャー	54	ナイン・ストーリーズ		☆☆☆
	71	ライ麦畑でつかまえて		☆☆☆
ウイリアム・サローヤン	84	パパ・ユア クレイジー		☆☆
エリック・シーガル	80	ラブ・ストーリィ		☆☆
アーウィン・ショー	38	夏服を着た女たち		☆☆
ズフェルト	136	星占いの本		☆☆
チャールズ・ディケンズ	53	クリスマス・キャロル		☆☆
コナン・ドイル	105	シャーロック・ホームズの冒険	■	☆☆☆
	152	シャーロック・ホームズの回想		☆☆☆
マーク・トウェーン	143	トム・ソーヤーの冒険		☆☆
P・L・トラヴァース	83	メアリー・ポピンズ		☆☆

著者	番号	タイトル		評価
C・W・ニコル	59	風を見た少年		☆☆
L・フランク・バーム	74	オズの魔法使い		☆☆
ラフカディオ・ハーン	107	怪談		☆☆☆
ピート・ハミル	58	ニューヨーク・スケッチブック		☆☆☆☆
J・M・バリ	43	ピーター・パン		☆☆
F・スコット・フィッツジェラルド	110	華麗なるギャツビー		☆☆☆
アラン・ブース	95	マクベス*		☆☆
アーネスト・ヘミングウェイ	73	老人と海		☆☆☆
O・ヘンリー	96	O・ヘンリー 短編集	🎧	☆☆☆
	151	O・ヘンリー 名作集		☆☆☆
マイケル・ボンド	160	くまのパディントン		☆☆
カースティン・マカイヴァー	132	聖書ものがたり*		☆☆
	139	聖書の名言集*		☆☆
	156	アルプスの少女ハイジ*		☆☆
	157	ガリバー旅行記*		☆☆
ラルフ・マッカーシー	39	イソップ物語*	🎧	☆
	49	アメリカ昔ばなし*		☆☆
	100	アラビアンナイト*		☆☆
	130	ギリシャ神話*		☆☆
A・A・ミルン	135	クマのプーさん		☆☆
	146	プー横丁にたった家		☆☆
サマセット・モーム	126	モーム短編集		☆☆☆
L・M・モンゴメリ	57	赤毛のアン		☆☆☆
	69	続・赤毛のアン		☆☆☆
トーベ・ヤンソン	138	たのしいムーミン一家		☆☆
	147	ムーミン谷の彗星		☆☆
アストリッド・リンドグレーン	159	長くつしたのピッピ		☆☆
キャサリン・ルビンスタイン	128	ラブレターズ		☆☆☆☆
ヒュー・ロフティング	150	ドリトル先生航海記		☆☆
ローラ・インガルス・ワイルダー	60	大草原の小さな家		☆☆
オスカー・ワイルド	75	幸福な王子		☆☆☆
小林与志 (絵)	7	マザー・グース	🎧	☆
	35	マザー・グース 2		☆
	122	マザー・グース 3		☆

日本の作品

著者	番号	タイトル	評価
赤川次郎	9	三姉妹探偵団	☆☆
秋月りす	112	OL進化論	☆☆
	149	OL進化論2	☆☆
芥川龍之介	27	蜘蛛の糸	☆☆
天樹征丸 (文)	129	金田一少年の事件簿：オペラ座館・新たなる殺人	☆☆
さとうふみや (絵)	137	金田一少年の事件簿：電脳山荘殺人事件	☆☆
	144	金田一少年の事件簿：上海魚人伝説殺人事件	☆☆

井伏鱒二	42	山椒魚	☆☆
梅村由美子	134	ケーキの本	☆☆
折原みと	68	夢みるように、愛したい	☆☆
川内彩友美 (編)	18	まんが日本昔ばなし	☆
	25	まんが日本昔ばなし 2	☆
	33	まんが日本昔ばなし 3	☆
	106	まんが日本昔ばなし 4	☆
	109	まんが日本昔ばなし 5	☆
	140	まんが日本昔ばなし：動物たちのお話	☆
北 杜夫	29	どくとるマンボウ航海記	☆☆
黒柳徹子	2	窓ぎわのトットちゃん	☆☆
小林まこと	117	ホワッツ・マイケル	☆☆
椎名 誠	77	岳物語	☆☆☆
高木敏子	21	ガラスのうさぎ	☆☆
太宰 治	36	走れメロス	☆☆
俵 万智	56	サラダ記念日	☆☆☆
夏目漱石	8	坊っちゃん	◉◉ ☆☆
	141	吾輩は猫である	☆☆
	158	三四郎	☆☆
新美南吉	114	ごんぎつね	☆
比嘉富子	155	白旗の少女	☆☆
星 新一	3	ノックの音が	☆☆
	22	きまぐれロボット	☆☆
	48	エヌ氏の遊園地	☆☆
松谷みよ子	10	ちいさいモモちゃん	☆
宮沢賢治	15	どんぐりと山猫	☆☆
	31	銀河鉄道の夜	☆☆
	78	風の又三郎	☆☆
村上春樹	12	1973年のピンボール	☆☆☆
	26	風の歌を聴け	☆☆☆
	51	ノルウェイの森 I	☆☆☆
	52	ノルウェイの森 II	☆☆☆
	62	羊をめぐる冒険 I	☆☆☆
	63	羊をめぐる冒険 II	☆☆☆
山田詠美	90	放課後の音符	☆☆
吉川英治	1	宮本武蔵 名場面集	☆☆☆
	148	新書太閤記 名場面集	☆☆☆
ラルフ・マッカーシー	153	日本の神話*	☆☆
	162	日本わらい話*	☆☆

講談社英語文庫 （カセット・セレクション） 楽しく聴いて英語が身につく

◉◉ 印のタイトルは、英文テキスト部分を録音したカセット・テープが発売されています。シリーズの中から人気作を選りすぐりカセット化しました。通勤・通学、家事の時間など、いつでもどこでも気軽に楽しめます。名作の朗読を聴くことにより、耳を英語に慣らすことができます。